Vital Signs

Edward Ragg

Published by Cinnamon Press
www.cinnamonpress.com

The right of Edward Ragg to be identified as author of this work has been asserted by him in accordance with the Copyright, Designs and Patent Act, 1988. © 2024, Edward Ragg
ISBN 978-1-78864-152-4

British Library Cataloguing in Publication Data. A CIP record for this book can be obtained from the British Library.

Designed and typeset in Bodoni by Cinnamon Press. Cover design by Adam Craig © Adam Craig.

Cinnamon Press is represented by Inpress.

Acknowledgements

'Final Diner at the Banquet of Dreams' appeared in a slightly earlier version in *Acumen* 105. 'A Second Body', 'Initiation Ceremony', 'Angel of the North', 'The Pulse' and 'Unfinished Symphony' were all published in *SAGINAW* 12.

The quotation from Firth et al.'s 'Interview with Jack Gilbert', which precedes 'The Invisible House', was originally published in *CutBank* Vol. 1. Issue 48 (1997) and is freely available.

The translation from Virgil's *Aeneid* Book VI, opening 'A Second Body', is my own.

Leslie Jamison's description of Raymond Carver used as an epigraph to 'The Diplomat' is quoted with permission from *The Recovering* by Leslie Jamison, copyright © 2018. Reprinted by permission of Little, Brown and Company, an imprint of Hachette Book Group, Inc.

The quotations preceding 'Angel of the North' derive from an interview with Antony Gormley freely accessible on YouTube at: https://www.youtube.com/watch?v=hmLBQtO8Od0

The quotations embedded in 'Angel of the North' derive from various newspaper articles of the time and comments in the sculpture's visitor book which are also reproduced in *Making an Angel* (London: Booth-Clibborn Editions, 1998/2000).

I would especially like to thank Jan Fortune and Adam Craig of Cinnamon Press for their continued support and origination of my work; as well as Maureen N. McLane, Claire Dyer, Eleanor Goodman, Alex Dougherty and Nazeer Chowdhury.

Contents

Vital Signs

I. Body

The Invisible House

There's a thing I heard about the bullfight I like which was the first thing a bull does when he comes out to the arena is find his home. You can't tell why. Each one will do it differently. He will go and stand in that place and will come out of there to deal with the toreador or the matador. He will get hurt and tired, and he will go back to his house. I love the idea of that invisible house.

~ Jack Gilbert (1997 interview, Firth et al.)

If not a house, then the bull of us
marking hooves in the fateful sand.
The whole arena staring through
what Oppen (after Williams) called
the little holes of our almost invisible
houses blinking naked at the world.

From where we ponder how
the Spanish named sand *arena*.
Word turned flesh like a foot in dirt.

We return to the body because
the fight is hard. You speak of
the many deaths to which the heart
succumbs panting in the afternoon sun.
Returning to that same spot as if
you had left the body purposely,
stomping fate into imagined ground.
Go back to your house.

Maybe it wasn't the bull or combat
or even the monstrosity of saying
the matador loves each beast he kills,
but the teasing to death that pretends
life's spectacle is a staring crowd.

So fate finds her inevitable feet.
But the body is not in love with death.
No, nor really the heart.

Or was it the mind slumping on
baked earth, fashioning Minotaurs

and the labyrinths to keep them
our darkest secrets from plain sight?

Maybe poetry is the body's other dance.
Flamenco duende made breath at last.

What is plain sight? The heart is
the invisible house where we return
exhausted and hurt. But we do return.
We stand our ground.

Dark artificer, never forget you have
no other lamp to light, no other
animal to master but dark sight.

A Second Body

Tum pater Anchises "animae, quibus altera fato
corpora debentur, Lethaei ad fluminis undam
securos latices et longa oblivia potant."

Then father Anchises said "They are spirits
destined to live a second life in the body.
They congregate here to drink from
the brimming Lethe and its water
heals their anxieties and destroys
all remnants of memory."

~ Virgil, *The Aeneid* (Book VI)

I had not thought to return alive
as the world burnt to ember and cinder
the coldest winter in living memory.
On the palate, a bittersweet after-
taste of Lethe's least potent shallows.
That flavour gone, a subtle mouthfeel
remains… like silken lees.

What system outage at Hades Inc.
allowed this exception to stroll almost
unnoticed through the gates of fate?

A second body, but the same. Young
again, if facing the mirror of middle age.
Memories of the first life, days lost
and that fateful pain in the chest.

Also, what should never have been
remembered. The ferryman's face wrinkled
with anger as another undead but unbidden,
ignoble too, dared muddy his waters.

The banks of souls—my father nowhere
to be seen—and indelible even to Lethe's
drops the frantic recoiling of those still weeping
at the feel of warm sand between their toes.

A second body still wet from the latest escape
out from the poet's wilderness of stars and woods
and whatever glorious unseen fields those were.

How we laugh to feel it leaping, lithe, unclean.

How It All Started

A soft American voice
speaking with the quiet

assurance of all the deep
-rooted trees of New England

having seen many a Fall
and the great Puritan sins

extending until now, their
long boughs swaying above

the butchered natives who'd
first inscribed this land

with poetry, painting and their
own ways of knowing things.

I was a sapling in transatlantic shade.
Collar and tie obscuring soft bark.

Grappling with words in the mouth
and signs on the page, their mutual

exchange. Later, listening to whole
bodies of poems echoing across

land and sea. Never bound to stay put
as their spines folded on themselves.

How these complete utterances
sounded out the very chambers

of the heart and cut across line by
line seething voices in the corridors.

How I wanted poetry to fall
like rain on young bark or as

certainly as the incoming tide.
Often denying my heart, as if

there were some right to wander
drunk at night through spired streets.

So many of us out of love
with ourselves but loving

someone or something else.
That was how it all started.

I return to that kind American
voice now dead to the world.

Embodying living ghosts
not erased selves. The Chinese

describe a drunk as 酒鬼
(*jiu gui*), an alcohol ghost.

Branwell Brontë brushing himself
out of his own portrait with Emily,

Anne and Jane. The presence of
his denial alive in each black daub.

Telling the dark hole in the soul from
which no light emits I told you so.

So in the quieter streets of now
I know not where it all started but how.

The Diplomat

A diplomat from the bleakest reaches of his own wrecked life.

~ Leslie Jamison on Raymond Carver

Forever on the road with no prospect
of arriving. His loyalty to that esteemed
spouse guaranteed unwavering fidelity.

Reeking in the grey morning light of stalled
talks, failures to negotiate, angry faces
forming the pursed lips of dry reprimands.

He thought this whole rhetoric uncivil.
The back and forth of jibes and requests
to leave immediately beneath his dignity.

Imagine his resistance to being searched
at bus and airport terminals when inside
the same diplomatic bag they found

the latest empties. For there is no outrage
besides the madness of gin. And no
preciser departure from anywhere known.

Only he was authorized, having travelled
for so many years across the wastes and
moss-hung recesses of his own wrecked life

to know the contents of that bag.
Only he appreciated in finest detail
the sense of waiting not to improve,

the delicious certainty of not being
committed to any greater power than
that dark spouse's dominatrix whims.

But in the end he mastered the subordinate.
Knowing his will more intoxicating,
more wilfully determined even than hers.

Now droplets of West Coast rain speckle
his grave. His late fragment a water-dappled
epitaph proclaiming how he'd got what

he wanted in the end. For who wouldn't want
to say I am beloved? To call one's self that?
To feel beloved in the moist Pacific air?

Body of Evidence

For over twenty years we've roamed the earth.
Its valleys, deltas, skies. The great body of it.

Sometimes hand in hand. Sometimes alighting
on tarmac in distant lands. From Huasco

to Cafayate to the Sicilian tides. Without touch
but with each return journey in heart or mind.

Love is not a map: unless its scale is one-to-one.
Like Borges's cartographic fun. And true it is

from love's valleys, deltas, skies, how hard
to see the outer limits or view from above

of the same hearts beating in parallel.
As perhaps two souls find they are not

stiff twin compasses whose arms are
always joined no matter where they roam.

My heart travelled too, trying to find
the better man who'd always lived inside.

Can I say in love we locate ourselves?
Perhaps you are right. No matter

what the day or anniversary tiding
we are still ourselves in our own way.

Traversing years without need
of demarcations or direction signs.

We are not the Douro's boundary stones
nor counter-signed proof of the once-betrothed.

So, we end where we began, stepping
out into the world's heart once more,

the body of evidence amassing
like swelling tides caressed by

the moon. The one-to-one of
journeys ended and journeys begun.

Initiation Ceremony

Translate the following:

Tempus est ad urbem regrediendi

It is time to return to the city.

Gladiatores pavati sunt et ad puguandum et ad moriendum

Gladiators are prepared both for fighting and dying.

Hostibus fortiter resistendo urbem servabimus

We shall save the city by resisting the enemy bravely.

Nulla spes erat ex oppido eo die effugiendi

There was no hope of escaping the town that day.

Diligenter audiendo multa et utilia disces

You will learn many useful things by listening carefully.

Puer festinando domum ante noctem pervenit

The boy reached home before night by hurrying.

So the boy sloughed off camouflaged fatigues
from aching limbs muttering unspeakable demotic.

Something about Lesbia's sparrow,
his body hardening in the ever-closer night.

Reflecting how you will learn many
useful things by listening carefully.

Angel of the North

My body is the only bit of the material world I inhabit.

Museums are hospitals for objects that cannot look after themselves.

~ Antony Gormley

Local press headlines of the day:

Nazi… but Nice? The Angel with a Dirty Face.
One commentator suggests: *String the artist up.*

The visitor book elaborates:

The birds will have somewhere to shit

and

Give it to London, because they're shite.

Memories of Tony Harrison's *V*
reversing the North South Divide.

Twenty-five years on the car park is packed.
Here on the pithead of the old Team Colliery.
Mine workings once swallowed a hundred
tonnes of grout to heave your seven hundred
tonne concrete throne. Unfearful symmetry:
each fifty-tonne wing arming your fifty-four
metre span. Hartlepool steel workers welded
these curvaceous legs and bulbous feet pinned
for perpetuity by fifty-two bolts embedded
three metres deep into that concrete plinth
merely to let you withstand the northern wind.

Today I return from years of flight to sense
the reverence in this inhuman breast. Standing
on, not above, the accumulated past beneath.
Men so blackened with soot only the whites
of their eyes could shine once washed at your feet
where the colliery bathhouse opened in 1939

as Europe burst into flame one more time.
Gormley called you an earthing device.
Fixing an angel here to ask if art can survive
its lightning visions by inhabiting the same
genius of the place. Your steel ribs housing
that darkness within like the inner workings
of all living bodies, blood and feeling hidden
from sight, only to return to the same elements.

I took first steps in this land of shoulders
and marching feet. Not certain of the fences,
too young for picket lines, but guilty still
somehow of standing to one side before
I knew no shame in looking askance,
in understanding the questioning stance.

My father still reads the dictionary every day.
He says your life depends on your power
to master words (Arthur Scargill, 10th Jan 1982).

Wherever I tread I recollect your steel wings
and ribbed legs bolted to this shale mound.
A necessary angel of permanent reality
not caught fleetingly for a moment standing
in the door but erected in actual space.

There is the body, the abstract body and
the abstract. None stranger to feeling
but of stranger feelings compressed.

Barely an hour from here my father toiled
in Billingham's chemical sites. I loved
the complete order of cooling towers
and piping flares, the language of
the elements codified in those tables
of numerical runes beyond my speech
before I knew my tongue could test
the fabric of things as they seemed.

The Angel stands. The headlines echo.
Somewhere an artist is strung, oscillating
like a moment's tuning fork, whilst elsewhere
the heartstrings vibrate in the hiss and smoke
of an old smelting works. Prometheus never
foresaw this burning age. I press 'Start'
and ignite the motor to carry me away
from this inflammable totem's stage.

Wondering am I, after all, inseparable
from declining tribes and darkening skies?

Standing Orders

Long corridors of the secluded schools,
distal pitches, a thousand darkened courts

flashing in the memory's eye as electric
grids flicker alight in febrile succession.

That was how things stood then.
Or how the world looked then.

But I am among the luckiest
of men only standing to order

in earlier lives. Bodies of bodies.
Shock of pubic hair, the pride of it.

Later, crossing lands and seas. How
the body lingers in New South Wales.

A young man standing on ancient soils
among sequestered eucalypt groves

considering fossils, fortune and
irrelevant goals. Trying, trying

so very hard (harder) to ignore
the standing orders but finally

falling by wrong ways. Not having
heard the body's remonstrance.

Its fine insistence on marginal
not partial truths. So that they

thought they were right to gloat
at the Icarus-gleam of failed wings

when they had only happened on
the truth by flying kites of fatality.

For years I kept hearing Ezekiel's last
stand in Blake's vast brightness of sight:

And is he honest who resists
his genius or conscience,

only for the sake of
present ease or gratification?

So we present ourselves at last.
Not standing in, but as bodies,

if a little late, at least here and
still at last in good standing.

O Body, O Teacher

How does the body teach?
The body I once ignored

or through good fortune
did not seek, did not ask

to explain my existence or
speak in my place as if this

vibrating coil were merely
some representative on earth

(but where else can we breathe?)
only later known as only own.

Each lyric poet knows not I.
Here where there is only you

and me and the poem between.
For the self is not the body

though we may not live anywhere
other than in these imploring limbs.

How much matter matters for the
unsolid self? Knowing no more no less?

The destruction of having to know.
Not because the knowledge destroys.

But its devouring is like a stomach
ingesting itself, like the autolysis of yeast.

As the Buddha says, what sort of man
shot by an arrow refuses treatment

until he knows who released the bow?
Or of what tree the bow was hewn?

The unhealable wounds of the must
be known are not the body's life.

It cures as well as age allows
and one day will cease to heal.

Perhaps there is an end of suffering when
the unseeable self accepts her shell.

Here where we can only live and know
the silent lessons of her dividing cells.

II. Pulse

Touching One

One touch was enough
for our two hearts

to hear each other
beating hard and fast.

But in truth
there was prelude

to that touch, as
I heard you singing.

And, listening, felt
a longing there.

But wondered
was the longing

for someone else
or someone lost

or merely my own
hope of longing.

Then one touch
was not enough.

Our two hearts
craving more than

the pulse of their
own beating.

For of that longing
there is no end.

Knowing there is
a softer song,

an even silent one,
only deepest lovers

sing in pulsing bodies
and craving hearts.

Where touching one
is touching many.

But touching you
is sweetest melody.

Unfinished Symphony

This slate-grey miniature British Shorthair
with eyes as amber as Riesling TBA

purrs with the pulsing crackle of firewood
echoing in the flickering hearth of her

chimney organ nose. The humming
pulse of contentment only a cat can sing.

I wonder too at her beating heart
inaudible beneath this tireless orchestration.

Silent conductor at whose baton's
flick she sets the varying tempo.

Considering how her exuberant chortles
on life recall Mongolian or Tuvan

throat singers, vibrating their vocal
cords to pitch not one tone but two.

Such chords of wonder, such double-
pitched harmonies as can make

one voice another like this cat's
insatiable duet of clarion and diapason.

How she revels in grateful frequencies.
The high flame of excitement soaring

above the burning embers of remembered
pleasure pulsing like double basses below.

There is no real language for her tones.
The French *ronronner* is not, *mes amis,*

a par on real purrs. The Chinese 猫叫
(mao jiao) says only the cat calls or cries

in the hutongs of her dark nights.
But purring is not calling.

Who can even name her genius
of embodied noises, yes, you,

Pedigree Purrer? Performing each day
with no coda it seems her unique,

unfinished symphony of peace.

Papers

Papers of no import papers
of import no longer of import
no papers of import retain retain

RETAIN

each capital etched in your
unmistakable hand, pointed graphite
pencil tip tearing through polymer
enveloped rectangulated retained

each cellophaned envelope sliced
open by the same blade corresponding
to that correspondence as per
the preceding correspondence
as per instructed as per as per
the envelope instructed retained

in envelopes of papers concerning
those actions of import on behalf
of those actions concerning papers
of non-action regarding the same
envelopes you write again again

ACTION REQUIRED

the required action enveloped
but of no import retained
though still of action required
for there are actions required
and required actions of import
requiring actions of no import

all dated dated enveloped and
dated the actions dated
the papers of no import dated
the papers of import no longer
of import dated

but the papers of import…?

Father, I hold your loosening hand
clasping mine as my pulse beats
now more quickly as I watch
your heart beat now more slowly
until I am holding your registered death
and its required causes in paper-cut hands.

The Pulse

The worldbeat Celan called it:
Welttakt. Coining the tokens,

the casino chips of a newly
minted transactional speech.

The gamble we take every time
we try to say what we think.

My phone buzzes and translates

沙子在沙面上行走…
The sand is walking on the sand.

A friend suggests this is the pulse.

Or what vibrates in someone's mind
imagining our each and every move.

The whole feeling of the world
where we too are beating.

Klee said a painting is
like a line taking a walk.

The poem is pulsing
in the late afternoon sun.

The sand is walking on
the sand of the world's heart.

The Dress

It shouldn't have been there
hanging in the wardrobe.

But had to be and needed
to be hung, you said.

Is it a life less lived
to be this uncreased?

I cannot argue with this dress.

For there is a certain field
or country lane on the less

cultivated banks of insanity
where someone remonstrates

with a dress. But the words
cease and I love the quiet

feel of the loose fabric always
speaking of its wearer as if

we could feel her whole form
embody its delicious contours.

Dress, no dress, you leave me
speechless time and again.

I almost feel the pulse in the very
veins of the seamstress who sewed

the exquisite lace and Korean pink
of this forever floating garment.

Speechless, almost breathless,
my heart slows, beating inside

the wardrobe where the dress still
hangs holding me forever close.

Heart of Hearts: The Pendulum's Beating

There is the feeling of the heart beating.
There is the feeling of the rhythm
of our hearts beating. And there is
the feeling of feeling. These three we feel.

Devices count time by the oscillation
of quartz. Their crystalline precision.
But there are no two clocks that can be
synchronized as your heart and mine.

In 1583, let's say it was Sunday 10th March,
Galileo attended Mass in the cathedral
in Pisa watching the great chandelier
swing gently to and fro as a priest
lit the first candles, then let it go.
No matter the weather or the incensed
words from the pulpit that day,
as the chandelier gently shortened
its swing the time it took to mark
its beats was always the same.

But how could he know? The teenager
counted his pulse watching the chandelier
always shift in seemingly changing pace
to the same time in space.

                        So you and I
incline to each other with the regularity
of two pendulum clocks. Across this city,
across mountains and sea, without speaking,
your heart speaks to me inaudibly because
our heart of hearts always beats the same.

Today I saw a discarded hazmat suit
abandoned in a basement carpark—
crumpled white-grey boot covers
trampled into the seat of its pants—
and thought *This is still our world.*

No matter the barricades, the wire fences,
the smartphone codes suddenly denying us,
the closing, the sealing of every door of every
locked-down compound of this perpetual now,
our hearts vibrate to the perfect calibration
of a love which says *But this is still our world.*

The Repairing

The lightning strike of anger
setting fire to the plains.

The plains are the heart
burning by the pulse of its flames.

We repaired to the pagoda of
the old park imagining ourselves

reunited. And from those
smouldering embers asked,

'Is this repairing? Is this
what repairing is?'

If the plains are the heart
and the anger ignites

the common grass and even
rarer plants, will they greet

the same sun next year?
Sprouting through

the rejuvenated earth in
the pulse of holding hands.

Maybe all couples part
in recombining hearts.

Maybe. Repairing to that
high hill overlooking the city.

Over the scorched plains
we can see the fire is out

for now. The last plumes
of smoke curling upwards

in the wintry air as if they
too can only be forgotten.

Calavera: For The Day of The Dead

I remember the skeletons
embracing in Santa Cruz,

Colchagua. How the eye
could not help but flesh out

the intimacies they held.
Unseeing the fruitless stare

of annihilation. How in
the airport in Santiago late

that night we laughed at the bar
called Last Stop Pisco Sour

but found ourselves supping
on the sweet strength of them,

roaring with laughter at
all the other skeletons who

couldn't keep their liquor
down (or up for that matter),

wondering what poems might
mark the day, any day really

except the last one, the last stop,
the last laugh in the bottom

of the glass whose terminal pulse
shattered in the cliché of all

blockbuster shootouts just about
every bottle and bone in that joint.

Everyone soused in Pisco Sour going
up so sweetly in neon-lime flames.

Flames flying over the noses
of all the parked aeroplanes.

And someone saying *This is
the joke of death, I guess*.

For it's not how you tell it.
You just had to be there to get it.

Final Diner at the Banquet of Dreams

Eight months of English sun and rain sifting
through the shadows of towering cumulus
billowing like ships' sails in the northern wind
have composted your remains in the uncaring earth.

Never had imagination so vividly and swiftly
transplanted me to that same spot where
I scattered you. In less than a heartbeat
considering the green turf our final picnic spot.

In dreams even more quickly returned, leaving
Beijing's volcanic hills for the forested slag heap
of an old mining village beneath Durham's skies
hedged into the ridged back of an old Roman road.

I have laid the table here a thousand times, knowing
the grass too wet for rugs and regret, preparing
roll-mop herrings, raw onion, gherkins, sour cream,
a frost-chilled glass of aquavit and carafe of golden wine.

Always I am serving you as an intimate who knows
he will join the feast when the appropriate time arrives.
Only later do I see I cannot break bread with the dead.
Not today at least. Besides, your soufflé has yet to rise.

We observe how well your ashes have melted away,
seasoning the great stock of the earth. Certain cheeses
are compared, accompanied by red-faced renditions
of the best Port vintages in your living memory.

Only when coffee arrives do you shift in your chair.
For eight months you rustled up this revolving banquet
of dreams. But as I let slip a cheery *Until next time*
you look sheepishly at your watch. The hands have stopped.

Suddenly your chair is gone. I am clearing plates,
scattering rinds for squirrels and birds, as a voice
keeps saying *Alas, how is't with you, that you do bend
your eye on vacancy?* But he was there, there, you see.

I am become an old butler employed by no one
holding discourse with the bodiless air. My pulse
racing like a drunkard's high jinks falling down
each and every nightmare's perpetual flights of stairs.

This is not madness. Bring me to the test and
I will recount what dreams these were and everything
you said that day. My heart beating more temperately
now, the picnic table folded, the grass green and bare.

First Breath

Before our lips touch
we inhale this first breath.

Our diaphragms lift.
Our abdomens contract.

Then each and every
molecule of vapour

exhaled embraces
the moist evening air.

Our lungs conduct this
dance of gaseous exchange.

And the heart?
Only the heart knows

what lips will touch.
The lips its emissaries.

Or maybe only the tongue
sends back word silently

to the heart. Of how it feels
to beat outside the body.

Then the heart may know
love is the consistent beat

that shares the pulse
of another body echoing.

The Bat and the Chair

How had she entered the old house?

A young navigator testing her
bearings in the echo-sense
of a warm September night.

Reluctant intruder, sweeping
through the back door or sashed
window left ajar to twilit fields.

I secured the internal doors as
she flickered in frantic, arced flight
on extended calcars. Then...

Momentary disbelief she'd been
reunited with dark-winged night.
But on the landing I found her

each third digit folded over her
exhausted wings panting for breath
on the chair by your vacant room.

So tiny in her resting state, her black
fox head, nose leaf and svelte ears slowing
to the inaudible tune of a recovery.

I tumbled downstairs to unlatch the old
oak door priests once heaved, glad she'd
already swooped past unheard and unseen.

Next morning you stopped breathing.
I recalled the young bat who'd visited
your old lair, yearning for significance,

doubting as it flew inaudibly past how
any Puritan in the heart could breathe
a word of how she was a type of heaven.

And yet somehow to this day I know
the little bat who lost her way that night was
harbinger of all last journeys and resting spots.

What remains. What is beyond remaining.
The rest is silence. How only the night
can hear the end of being echoing.

The Denial Artist

As a boy I visited a painter
who spoke of Gurdjieff

and the poetry of Yeats
in the same breath.

In the cool grey light
of the old stone house

one hot summer's day
in an English school town

he told me how Yeats
once suffused an entire

carriage as if by magic
with the bouquet of roses.

The boy in my heart rolled
on the carpet and howled.

The sheer silliness of it.
My heart smelt my body

rolling in the mould and
dust of that moth-eaten rug.

But I perched on my chair and
listened patiently, watching

Yeats in his carriage winking
through spectacles, talking

of sudden odours in his pocket
or in the palms of his hands.

Later, flush with homemade wine,
I stumbled down the winding stair.

The old oak door was portal
to ordinariness and school.

But suddenly in the corridor
anticipating humid, cut-grass air

incense and potpourri, dried
roses, lavender, Earl Grey tea.

But no painter nor poet
stood at that threshold.

What choice had I?
I denied the undeniable.

Became the denial artist
the painter worried I'd be.

Then, with time, the odour of
his anecdote faded quietly away.

But thirty years on, I place
this glass of wine to one side

to summon that painter's mind.
The jasmine of my heart to hand.

Walking back up the winding stair
as a gyre opens through phases

of the moon. Seeking words like
dried roses. Suddenly fragrant again.

Windbreak

The viticulturalist levels her eye
on leafy canopies, mint green foliage,
considering the gusts that disappoint
flowering and fruit-set *down the line*.
The great Cape Doctor's tutelage.
I place my frame within yours that
the winds of heaven may not visit
your face too roughly. Gobi corridors
through which my spirit trains within
the trellising wires of a mortal coil.
On my walk to work the Beijing wind
prophesies the future gales that will
buffet my grave. But I will have no grave.
And not speak gravely. Only hoping
one day to be cast to the wind perhaps
here on Chinese earth, lain to rest in
the street outside some Chengdu noodle
shop where I'll look back fondly on
Sichuan girls and languishing men
having their ears cleaned in the tea-soaked
hours as though this were the best time
to laugh at death. The vast Sichuan
mountains weaved from the Tibetan plateau
will hem me in from all blustery ends.
Or maybe sods of Durham earth will
contain my silence in secret, dark fertility.
Breaking my fall into eternity. Enough.
For it is enough to feel my bear-like mass
has made your own universe one degree warmer.
Less blown away by the sheer scale of things.

The Calling

A flurry of autumn leaves, now yellow,
now red, pressing against the classroom's
windowpanes where the words on the page
seemed to breathe in the world beyond them.

Soft yellow sunlight clearing the path
through those leaf-etched shapes, arriving
at hundreds of thousands of miles per second
into the arms of those still echoing sounds.

For only there could the calling be heard.
Not bellowed from mountaintop nor gasping
at twitching hazel in the autumn fog. Electric,
yes, but no pulsing diviner's rod. It was like

a chord sustained and sustaining where
the breath of whispering vowels and plucky
consonants sounded out the same heart
they had always sought. Or seemed to seek.

Or maybe the heart found in those very pages
the unfamiliar announcement of its own
recognition, where no mythological harp
sang in god-given breath or fantastic ensemble.

I hear the same calling in the leaves of
a second life, in the beauty of all second lives.
Where the calling is chosen not choosing.
The gusts and heavy breaths of the first life

casting no shadow on the page before us
but living in memory of that choice. For to speak
now in a voice assured and assuring is no
betrayal of pain. We are merely opening

the window again. Undoing the latch in the heart
to let in the leaves and wetter hours of afternoons
lost and mornings recovered. Rediscovering in
the first light a second wind echoing the calling.

Marco Polo and the Snowflake

In the quarantine hotel, I lift the lid
of the unpolished brass spyhole
embedded in my bedroom door.
Yellow light looks in. Only on
dropping finger and thumb do I see
this camera obscura's shutter
is debossed MARCO POLO.
As if his ghost beamed on the floor.

Outside, Beijing snows. The gingko
sway: one green, one yellow, one
considering orange days. Later, the wind
will rise as packed snow confronts
the greenest gingko calling yellow and
orange witnesses to its annual demise.
But what is one year in the life of a tree?

I look through the glass like a Venetian
in Murano whose life is elsewhere.
The glass-blower's breath enlarging
a snow globe of some forbidden city as
magical as Polo's tales of Kubla Khan.
His heart floating midway on the waves
between buried city and pleasure dome.

The latch on the window is loose,
but the chain strong. I can hear planes
skidding off ice at Da Xing and
your breath condensing across the city,
where in that crystalline garden you catch
snowflakes quietly in your hand.

Perhaps I am incapable of seeing Venice.
Or can glimpse only a gondola stuck in ice
or citadel frozen in glass beneath the waters.
We pray for glacial weather so you may
cross the frigid laguna and take my hand.
But, though in love, this is not our city.

Here our blinking phones illuminate
the passageways between us as a billion
shutters open and close. Can I say
my chained window is ajar, the room
held on ice for your arrival? Do we
care who is looking in or why? And if
I open the lid again will we see Polo's
love untying her silk brocade outside?

All impossible as Venice in a Beijing light.
They will never believe you came this way,
shaking their heads in the thawing night.
They will never believe you alighted
in my hand fresh from a snowflake borne
on the breath of this November wind.

Some say I told this tale to Marco
centuries ago and oft he repeated it
in the hostile passageways of that
amorous city. Some say.

I say your breath is the wind that
buoys me, that incredulity melts
quickest at the heart's open core.

It was no dream, no miracle they saw
as they spied through the keyhole or
bolted the convex lens from the door.

A stranger seating a snowflake in the
bow of an icy gondola that flew away.

Osmanthus Days

I was the child of those garden years.
Barely taller than rose bushes, breathing
their occasional fragrance in the now
backlit memory of golden flowered days.
I remember deep brown soil crumbling
in tiny hands and a man who came
to build a wall, my friend pulling me
away impatiently to play as I countered
No, I might learn something here.
The bricklayer smiling and setting
to silently with spirit level and trowel.

In Shanghai's August streets the osmanthus
blooms. Pungent lychee, melon and guava,
floral notes. The wine taster's terms failing me.
Yet I drink their bouquet.

                      Other words falter too.
But how else can I speak of the moon goddess
Chang'e? Osmanthus unveiling her perfume,
unspinning the yarn of how her pet jade rabbit
Yutu pilfered the lunch of the immortal Wu Gang.

And I am smiling now as much at how
these unwholesome divines required
three meals a day as how a jade rabbit
made off with such immortal tuck and why.
But still my nose wonders if Wu Gang's
lunch pail was perfumed with osmanthus buns.

And I am hungering too in these moon-lit
streets, my heart chasing rabbits, considering
the classical scholars sitting imperial exams
on humid August Suzhou days. To be admitted
to those high-scented ranks, they say, was to have
plucked the osmanthus from the Moon Palace.

Am I cavalier of attainment now? I have walked
so many steps but know of no ladder to the moon.
My childhood bricklayer built a wall that stands
today. But there is another knowledge breathing
beneath and through all walls as harmoniously
as the spirit-levelled edge of upstanding ends.

The osmanthus of your calling heart breathes
through me, speaking of Shanghai days or, as
a little girl, playing in the water towns, never
needing to say *No, I might learn something here.*

Memory backlit that golden garden, now my door,
whose scents mingle with osmanthus flowers
like walking into the foyer of a thousand
perfumed hotels. The foyer where our scents
collect in the same air of the palatial moon.

There Alongside

Death does indeed reveal itself as a loss, but a loss such as is experienced by those who remain. [...] The dying of Others is not something which we experience in a genuine sense; at most we are always just 'there alongside'

~ Heidegger, *Being and Time* (47: 282)

The unchanging nouns of the place.
Corridored, departmentally arranged.
There alongside in wards, recovery rooms.

But the adjectives changed. Medical bed.
Hospital bed. Sick bed... Death bed.
The finality of those unuttered

monosyllables carried in our hearts.
A leaden spondee at the end of the line
...

I want no portion of regret, memories
of almost lovers, nights lost to drink.
I want no rage either against the dying
of the light, though there may be anger.

After sifting papers (the official death
certified and signed) I long for days
in memory of your smile, playing jester
to our mother's hand, your childish delight.

Grief is the crosswind that buffets
life's tailwinds. We are merely navigators
trusting to sense and equipment more
or less accurate, if sometimes on the blink.

Finding our way between earth and sky,
comparing notes with those there alongside
until we close our eyes or simply see no more.

Until that time in the fading light
we find our own most ceasing to be.

Circular Breathing

We took deep breaths and advanced
on the garden holding each other as we went.
I stowed the makeshift urn between bicep
and clavicle, surprised at its weight, pausing
for breath as the wind wetted our eyes
already liquid in the bright afternoon light
of Durham skies. Autumn leaves skipped
across the verdant lawn as we reached
the vegetable patch, grassed over when it'd
become too much for you, or just too much.
Recalling gluts of courgette and once proud
artichokes surveying the cemetery over the fence.
Father, we will not commit you to hallowed ground,
knowing you consecrated this plot with love,
leeks and the chemical sense of every element.
For a moment I smile at how the deep green
of this unintended lawn is nitrogen rich.
Here where compost and manure married
macro- and micro-nutrients beneath our feet
and sustained our bodies too. The wind gets up.
I open the urn, conscious the world's breath
will one day scatter us as I sieve through the air
your final bonds: phosphates, sulphates, calcium salts.
Forming a circle—no, you correct—an oblate sphere.
And I am breathing more heavily now, though the load
is lighter, as if the wind drew the oxygen out our lungs
as this final oblation replaces the last breaths of words
and what we'd thought to say in remembrance
as I remember suddenly your incredulous look
as I failed to explain Wynton Marsalis's circular
breathing returning my childhood trumpet to its case
and recalling all those Remembrance Sundays playing
'Last Post' in the assorted villages of a chocolate-box
England which never breathed light of day anywhere
but in the hearts of those dead soldiers epitaphed
over the fence but their bodies in Flanders wishing
I could inhale now the molecules we are exhaling
and reoxygenate each and every heart that is grieving
as in the circle of your ashes I pledge to live as if
each moment were punctuated with our last breaths.

9 781788 641524